WHERE SHE HAS BEEN

poems by

Elva Lauter

Finishing Line Press
Georgetown, Kentucky

WHERE SHE HAS BEEN

ACKNOWLEDGMENTS

Phoebe: "Peach Blossom Moon Gate"
Porcupine: "The Peacock Tree"

Publisher: Leah Maines
Editor: Christen Kincaid
Cover Art: Great Mosque, Kairouan, Tunisia, by Hal Lauter
Author Photo: Drewcilla Annese
Cover Design: Elizabeth Maines McCleavy

Printed in the USA on acid-free paper.
Order online: www.finishinglinepress.com
           also available on amazon.com

Author inquiries and mail orders:
Finishing Line Press
P. O. Box 1626
Georgetown, Kentucky 40324
U. S. A.

Table of Contents

To Drewcilla,
a wonderful and helpful friend

Waiting Room

Between planes among other travelers
arriving, leaving
she plays recollections,
tries to read faces
but can't translate them,
her phrase book forgotten.

Before she arises and goes
to Katmandu, Alexandria, Yerevan,
she sniffs the rich scent of possibility,
bottles it for later,

but when she arrives
lost in a bazaar, a labyrinth of dim alleys,
shopping bag in hand,
she stumbles on cobblestones
searching for something, someone
she has yet to find.

Traveling the Silk Road

Place to place
golden spider paying out
silken lines—
she ascends
descends
mountain's climb,
fog-drenched Chinese forests.

Always behind
that telltale sign,
moth of midnight blue,
wrapped cocoon
scarab for luck.

Raindrops shake
from crystal web
at the hub
of silent wheel.
She waits for vibration
tune from thread
or call of muezzin
in high tower.

Moon
hangs from hibiscus,
pomegranate-red
in Samarkand—
next to Tamerlane's tomb
or in bazaar where she ponders
piles of pale-green melons.

At journey's end
she leaves behind
honey comb, sun-bright grapes,
squeezes the last drop
to sweeten her passage
back to a barren land.

Last Resort

She supposed she came here for vacation
late in thirsty summer
to this place of rusted pipes,
fifties furniture,
where she spends her time
trying on thoughts like bathing suits
that don't quite fit.
She thinks, "Nothing blooms in a desert,
not even desire."
or "I need endless, emptied stretches
of sand that profess nothing."

No film in her camera—
though she has plenty of pictures
of Fez and Samarkand,
other places of worn-out promises
that whisper dark romance,
light-hearted lovers
that always disappear over the horizon
with any sunset.

She needn't dress for dinner,
for barefoot, sunburned,
She has chucked all baggage,
remains by the pool.

No use for map or guidebook,
She has finished her trek
where dates are for gathering,
camels drink long at the watering hole,
has found her oasis.

Where She Has Been

In Zanzibar she sat
in a covered truck,
stared at rain
turning red dust to mud,
turning her thoughts to the running boy,
holding over his head,
a large, green palm leaf.

She bought a little round basket
of spices—cloves, cinnamon, chili
colored brown, tan, and rust—
plain sober colors
for such vibrant promises.

The spices are at home now
still covered with cellophane, unopened.
She picks the basket up,
turns it slowly in her hands.

From her window
she watches the downpour
drenching the cacti
in their red pots.

A leaf, a scent, a pot—
she counts them,
one, two, three...
The sky whispers with rain.
She always comes back
to where she has been.

Peach Blossom Moon Gate

(to Xue Tao, a Tang Dynasty woman poet)

In Chengdu she walks
into a Chinese painting
along a tiled wall
through the red stone moon gate,
under the peach tree
where blossoms fall
like pale stars.

Around her,
the bamboo garden quivers
with spring.

Xue Tao strolled here
through this green she loved,
drew water from this well,
made her own paper
on which she wrote her poems,
each character like the legs of cranes,
black against a dove-gray sky.

Peach petals float
in the pond of her palm.
Wind whispers
among bamboo leaves.

The Last of the Real Scarf Dancers

Danced through half of Europe—
Poland, Bulgaria, Romania,
Russia,
dashed up/down train aisles,
towel at the ready,
had the band play
gypsy music in Suzdal—
she was free.

When the bus driver danced,
kicking his legs out,
she waved her shawl over his head,
changed him into a cabbage
at midnight,
left with both glass slippers
and a bottle of vodka.

Standing on a balustrade
over a canal in St. Petersburg,
she twirled her scarves—
and she has pictures to prove it.

Showing others how,
flourishing a red cloth
to say good-by,
she did what she could...

Isadora would have loved her.

Mata Hari Blues

Slinking
through the left-hand doorway
of a Shanghai temple,
she huddles under a humpbacked peach bough
in a red lacquer court
where the black bat of happiness
hangs from a beam.

Grey-sky gazing,
spinning brocade robes,
clouds with no seams

in mandarin orange,
three pearl pendants on blue string.
She watches fish, crabs, crayfish
swimming near the ceiling.

Rain floods the courtyard
into her shoes.

Caught here
loverless,
umbrellaless,
no taxi in sight,
she betrayer is betrayed
by stabs
of icy showers.

Deluge drowning
a lost afternoon.

Sand Castles

In Arabian nights,
Malibu days,
she builds
shining palaces of sand,
constructed in an hour,

Bluebeard's castle
with scarlet rooms,
Moorish castle in Granada
blazing with sunlight,
Chinese heavenly palace
in peach-blossom afternoon,
moonlit castle
where she climbs towers,
lets dark-hair down
for evening to climb.

On battlements
where she hears waves
crashing,
behind casements,
where she watches
cormorant-wings,
shadows on water,

she loiters, waiting,
until the tide comes in.

Ceremony of Waves

She wants to return
to that place,
the beach in Mexico,
where green waves billow
almost to the door.
She hears them washing,
rinsing the sand white
while the sun dries,
burns glassily
beneath bare feet.

That evening,
at the restaurant, they eat fish.
She thinks of floating
in seaweed,
surprised by the rising moon,
the hum of stars.

Walking back to the cabin,
her skin remembers,
her lips part.
She tastes the plum-ripe night.

Dark Side

In Madagascar
she hiked along the path
to the waterfall
through tangled foliage
where vines strangled
trees; now and then
blood-red flowers spattered
the green.

On the way back
she saw the lemurs,
round eyes in fox-like faces
peering from among the leaves.
They startled her,
so unexpected.
Aren't they nocturnal?

Afterwards, remembering
how their long, ringed tails
slid silently
down the tree trunks,
she knew she'd been on the dark side
of a moon.

A Dog's Day at Machu Picchu

The dog appears
in his sculptural fatness
in the sun,
stretched out,
a long bag of brown flour
relaxed on the stone.

He seems asleep
except for one eye
open,
an ancestor
of other Incan dogs,
has been here always
part of these green terracotta hills.

Standing
on this observatory,
she wonders if she'll ever return
at midnight,
an Inca princess
in flame-red robe,
lover gone,
gates locked,
compelled to dance forever
to a far flute.

Her shadow shivers
on the rock;
the dog growls in his sleep.

In Istanbul

She wanders dark alleys
where swarthy men are shadows
chasing the last rays
of spent daylight
and women with veiled thoughts
glide through souks
as silently as moths
drawn to flame.

She wears silver beads
bought in the bazaar
which she fingers constantly
trying to remember where,
why she is here
looking for the Blue Mosque
in the white heat
of a dead day.

Mecca and Points East

It's a place she has read about—
white shadows on minarets
where the sun rubs
against noon walls
before sliding past the Great Mosque
into the market
to fondle, warm-fingered,
scarlet pomegranates, lush green melons.

She will pack and go then
to this lost/found city.
At the end,
she will find herself already there,
a red sun bursting
through her skin,
eyes flashing stars
in a daylight sky,
lips murmuring this poem,
her call to prayer,
her mantra against the scorching dark.

The Peacock Tree

The last night in Lisbon,
she climbs the hill
to the ruined garden,
enters a gate cracked with time.
A pair of swans skims
in a circle of pond.
Three geese hiss softly—
red beaks their signature
against the grass.

Looking to the left,
she sees the twilight tree
filled with peacocks,
feathery tails hanging
over branches
like bright veils.
This is where
they live their evenings.

Her hair stirs like feathers
in the wind—
this hour before moonlight

As night devours the light,
she hurries down the hill,
hears their cries
piercing the dark,
taking over the world
behind her.

Painted Desert Dancing in Mirage

She is living
Gobi Desert-style–
shaggy camel hair,
shadow-eyed,
lips drawn back
in perpetual smile,
always waiting
for the next oasis,

slaking thirst at brackish well–
forever crossing, re-crossing
salt/bitter sands under
a lemon-green sky
casting black shadows
around her bony legs,

setting up flimsy tent
in a high wind
among desolate dunes
on a caravan
to nowhere.

Blue Moon

She goes on safari
in the desert.
The wild rabbits
notice her flying hair
surrounding her.
It would feather their nest
if they had one.

At twilight, under the sky,
she gazes up.
Stars shine down,
sprinkling the air with light.

She turns to the blue moon.
Raising her arms,
she grasps it,
throws it back.

It is gone too soon,
like an old tune
she heard long ago.

Journey

She has been traveling
the narrow road to the deep north,
a back road to a far town.

Scraps of her life,
swallow flight moving on,
cutouts blown
across a paper sky.

She tries to read roadmaps,
decipher signposts pointing
in other directions,
catalysts for a new reality—
beyond the dust,
potholes, fallen rocks, dead birds,
lies another horizon

where a stream flows quietly
over black stones.

Looking Past the Light

All afternoon she sits
in this room,
the day distilled
into rain spilling
       down windows.

The familiar becomes habit
like a bird that spends
most of its life
on just one branch,
       flying
off now and then,
coming up for air
on a rumor
       of spring.

The horizon, with a twitch
of an eyelid
bleaches white, fades.
In the half light,
her leaf memory
       flutters,
drifts down river.

Tell her where to shed
this skin, this feathery blueprint.
She will fly in that direction.

Earth-Sister

O'Keeffed
into shell and bone
petal on petal
soft on hard,

peacock blue and gold
plumage beckons
the far nearby
desert flower
blown sky-wide,

she drowns in iris-eyes
well-black
no vein or blemish
mountain to stone,

dwelling in adobe
skull bleached bald
sockets stripped
ears echo cliff and hill,

she whispers
"spare, lean"
uncluttered.

Deserted Beach House

Salt on her tongue
this wind-whittled day
blows her over a lone stretch of summer
to the house at the edge
of the world,
sandy, sea-whipped
above the beach
where zig-zag trees
are clipped by wind.

She slips
into the shadowed cottage,
feels the night surge from corners.
Through a broken glass
she finds the sea—
blued, softly muttering
over its rosary of rocks and shells—
empty rooms,
footsteps echoing summer.

She doesn't know who lived here
or when,
yet she knows she must return,
beckoned by whispers,
"Come again, again."

For a shiver of time
she owns this place,
each dark and weathered board
hers.
She'll return to this empty house,
compelled once more to enter
and reenter.

The door creaks on its hinges,
a scent of lavender drifts in.

Leave the Balcony Open
(for Garcia Lorca)

Beneath a madder moon
where black shadows hover
by the fountain,
where dark doves rise
from leafless branches
and orange trees are barren
in Granada.

You are there
your eyes full of wings—
in morning,
evening,
at five o'clock
in the afternoon,
always green
always you
always there
always.

Country Bridge

It's been moved
to this place,
this wooden bridge,
fresh paint gleaming
in the hot Iowa sun.

She walks over it,
passing from here to there,
beginning and ending
near the parking lot.

But she remembers another bridge
when she rode in a car
through a green-jade day,
through a shaded tunnel.

She's seen it again in dreams,
light falling like rain
among trees at the end—
lost somewhere in Oregon
on a winding country road.

Stepping onto the pavement,
she drowns in the flood of light.

Here's Looking at You

Sipping a beer
at the Blue Moon,
she asks Dan to play it again.
Heard that tune before
along the boulevard;
it's checkmate
and recapitulation.

We walked, talked
of war, other times,
faces.
Your hand
in a gesture
of goodbye/hello
was, is–
has asked herself
a thousand times.
She still doesn't know.

She left on the train,
saw you dwindle to a speck.
Was it yesterday
we laughed
in the dim bar
in Tangier, Paris,
Madrid, Buenos Aires?

She is still waiting
under the elms
for a streetcar
named Dream, Hope,
Goodtimes.

Her pocket change clinks together
like strangers on a Mexican bus,
destination uncertain.

Oysterville

Here at the sea edge,
she shakes seaweed in its pool,
watches crabs run scribbly
in the sand
while all the black skies of rock turn
with their starfish.

With the windy sighs of summer,
the houses lost along the bay,
are empty in their burning;
all the startled shrubs stand up
waving in the sand.

Mountains of oyster shells
lie cracked, white in their sleeping,
exposing to the sun
their tidy, tender marrow,
their echoes of pools,
salty and dark
where they can go no more.

By the weathered oyster house
all the sad sands of summer
turn salted, wet with tide;
the shell of her being comes
pearl and part of that briniest foam
as she stands in the sun in a dream
of morning, oysters opened
and gone.

Puerto Barrios

She fell for him
on a ripe-banana day
yellowed in hot jungle sun.

Motel room
baked
with odor of cemetery rot,

no air conditioner
nor opening
to torpid street.

She a wilted moth
plastered against
the one light bulb.

He removed his shirt.

Far away
the last ferry belched,
gasped,
heading for Livingston
across the bay.

Outside
a ragged palm
clutched at the door.
She said,
"I can't stand this heat."
The manager replied,
"Es el trópico, señora,"
and left.

Later
an old fan
banged all night,
its flames
scorching their bare skin
till morning came
with no relief
and the night lay wasted
on the steaming floor.

Suddenly Summer

At the cocktail party she stands
in the corner and talks.
She has a third eye in the middle
of her forehead,
can see three things at once.
He has a shrimp on his tie,
and a green olive between his teeth.
She holds tight to her glass,
keeps her fingers crossed.

The clock strikes seven.

He asks,
"What have you been up to this summer?"
She says,
"It's rainy in Hokkaido."
Foxes slip by like ghosts through the mist
from the hot springs.
She leans on the railing,
watches people disappear along the path,
but she's back now and her shoes pinch.

She still smells the Sulphur.

Burnt Siena

Russet roofs, matte-rose walls, mustard domes—
raw umber, viridian green, yellow ochre,
summer music
slipping through corridors, out windows
over flagstones, up/down
in/out of mazes
becoming a pearl of sound
in the shell of the piazza;

from the top of the cathedral
listening angels trying their wings,
Madonnas nodding their heads
(keeping century time)
while all the saints come filing in—
freed unicorns dancing on frescoed ceilings
paintings spotting walls;

pigeons bowing near the palazzo,
the old sitting on benches
poring over the illuminated pages
of the sunset,

out the city gates
the Tuscan hills striped with vines,
accented with olive trees,
brushed with shadows—
she is burnt with sienna.

Saddle Mountain Blues

Leaving the ranch
she goes for a dream walk
up the winding trail
awash with pine cones,
cavorting squirrels,
bouquets of mushrooms.

Fir trees shelter her.
Moss and bark,
part of the whole,
envelop her
all afternoon.

When she reaches the saddle,
she will ride deep
into the blue.
As the red sun sets,
her hair turns blue.

She will fly
with the emerging stars;
stars in her blue eyes
glow and grow bluer.

Yucatan Night

All night the heat gathers, hovers
in the room.
Outside, tarantulas,
big as teacups, scramble
down the walls from the thatched roof,
along the cement porch,
seeking water.

Across the way, pyramids slumber
by moonlight. One of them,
an observatory, empty and open to the stars,
waits for Mayan priests to scan
the sky's midnight eye.
They must do this
before dawn, so they can map the day.

Tomorrow, she'll go there,
look for signs on stones.
Her path will be crossed by lizards.
The sun will burn tattoos into the ground.

Tonight, she'll dream of rain.

Castle

Red sandstone castle carved
in cliff, hanging in air,
no way up, no way down.

Eagles, black slashes sweep
across cobalt sky;
below—gray-oak limbs, bare bones
where openings appear—square, oblong,
curves, angles. What's inside?
Shadows playing—light, dark;
ladders gone, people gone—
no longer a way in or out.

It's dream time, corn god;
dance the rain in—
blue flute, gray flute,
ghostling in the early
morning.

Listen—
hear the raindrops
on the yucca leaves?

Elva Lauter was born in Astoria, Oregon, and lived there on the west coast until she left for college. She writes of her thoughts and feelings about many places she visited nearby, more widely throughout the United States, and abroad.

She has both a Bachelor's and Master's degree in English from the University of Oregon, and she worked on a Ph. D. at the University of Washington, where she met and married her husband of more than 60 years. They have long lived in the Los Angeles area of California, where she was an English professor at Glendale College, until retiring in the 1990s.

Together they have traveled to more than 100 countries in every continent except Antarctica. Her poetry reflects these visits and the places special to her. Her experiences in these locales and of the culture of the people there, as well as her great love of nature, find their way again and again into her writings.